Delaware Bingo Book

A Complete Bingo Game in a Book

DECEMBER 7, 1787

Written By Rebecca Stark

ISBN 978-0-87386-501-2

Educational Books 'n' Bingo

Printed in the U.S.A.

DIRECTIONS

> List of Terms
>
> Templates for Additional Terms and Clues
>
> 2 Clues per Term
>
> 30 Unique Bingo Sheets (To cut out or copy)
>
> Sheet of Markers (to copy and distribute)

1. **Either cut apart the book or make copies of ALL the sheets. You might want to make an extra copy of the clue sheets to use for introduction and review. Keep the sheets in an envelope for easy reuse.**

2. Cut apart the call sheets with terms and clues.

3. Pass out one bingo sheet per student. There are enough unique sheets for a class of 30.

4. Pass out the markers. You may cut apart the markers included in this book or use any other small items of your choice. Students can also mark the sheets themselves; recopy the sheets as needed for additional games.

5. Decide whether or not you will require the entire sheet to be filled. Requiring the entire sheet to be filled provides a better review. However, if you have a short time to fill, you may prefer to have them do the just the border or some other format. Tell the class before you begin what is required.

6. There are 50 terms. Read the list before you begin. If there are any terms that have not been covered in class, you may want to read to the students the term and clues before you begin.

7. There is a blank space in the middle of each sheet. You can instruct the students to use it as a free space or you can write in answers to cover terms not included. Of course, in this case you would create your own clues. (Templates provided.)

8. Shuffle the sheets and place them in a pile. Two or three clues are provided for each term. If you plan to play the game with the same group more than once, you might want to choose a different clue for each game. If not, you may choose to use more than one clue.

9. Be sure to keep the sheets you have used for the present game in a separate pile. When a student calls, "Bingo," he or she will have to verify that the correct answers are on his or her sheet AND that the markers were placed in response to the proper questions. Pull out the sheets that are on the student's sheet keeping them in the order they were used in the game. Read each clue as it was given and ask the student to identify the correct answer from his or her sheet.

10. If the student has the correct answers on the sheet AND has shown that they were marked in response to the *correct questions,* then that student is the winner and the game is over. If the student does not have the correct answers on the sheet OR he or she marked the answers in response to *the wrong questions,* then the game continues until there is a proper winner.

11. If you want to play again, reshuffle the sheets and begin again.

Have fun

TERMS INCLUDED

Atlantic Coastal Plain

Battle of Cooch's Bridge

Belemnite(s)

Blue Hen(s)

Border (-ed)

Civil War

Climate

Constitution

Counties

Crab(s)

Delaware Diamond

Delmarva Peninsula

Dover

Du Pont

Highest Point

Executive Branch

Flag

Thomas Garrett

Governor

Greenwich Loam

Grey Fox

Holly

Industry (-ies)

Judicial Branch

Lady Bug(s)

Legislative Branch

Lewes

Middle Atlantic

Milk

Motto

New Castle

Nickname

Caesar Rodney

Peach

Peach Blossom

Piedmont

River(s)

Seal

Sillimanite

Song

Stonefly

Strawberry (-ies)

Sweet Goldenrod

Three Lower Counties

Tiger Swallowtail

Underground Railroad

University of Delaware

Weakfish

Wilmington

Winterthur

Additional Terms

Choose as many additional terms as you would like and write them in the squares. Repeat each as desired.
Cut out the squares and randomly distribute them to the class.
Instruct the students to place their square on the center space of their card.

Clues for Additional Terms

Write three clues for each of your additional terms.

1. 2. 3.	1. 2. 3.
1. 2. 3.	1. 2. 3.
1. 2. 3.	1. 2. 3.

Atlantic Coastal Plain 1. Except for a small area in the north, most of the state lies in this geographic region. 2. This region is flat and seldom rises more than 80 feet above sea level.	**Battle of Cooch's Bridge** 1. The ___ was a battle of the American Revolution. 2. The Battle of Cooch's Bridge was the first action of the Philadelphia Campaign of the American Revolution.
Belemnite(s) 1. ___ is the common name for an extinct order of mollusks belonging to the cephalopod class. Modern cephalopods include the squid and octopus. 2. The ___ is the state fossil. ___ fossils are found along the Chesapeake and Delaware Canal.	**Blue Hen(s)** 1. The ___ is the state bird. The symbol goes back to the American Revolution when Delaware soldiers were compared to these birds for their fighting ability. 2. University of Delaware's athletic teams are called the Fightin' ___.
Border (-ed) 1. These states ___ Delaware: New Jersey, Pennsylvania, and Maryland. 2. Delaware is ___ by the Atlantic Ocean and Delaware Bay.	**Civil War** 1. Delaware stayed in the Union during the ___, but its citizens were divided in their loyalties. 2. Delaware was one of four slave states that did not secede during the ___.
Climate 1. Delaware has a temperate and humid ___. 2. Delaware's ___ is moderate year round.	**Constitution** 1. On December 7, 1787, Delaware, became the first state to ratify the United States ___. 2. Delaware is called The First State because it was the first to ratify the ___.
Counties 1. Delaware has three ___. 2. From north to south Delaware's three ___ are New Castle, Kent, and Sussex.	**Crab(s)** 1. The horseshoe___ is the state marine animal. There are more horseshoe ___ in Delaware Bay than any other place in the world. 2. ___ and clams are the state's most important seafood products.

Delaware Bingo

Delaware Diamond
1. The ___ is the name of the state star. It is the first star on the International Star Registry to be registered to an American state.
2. The ___ is located in the constellation of Ursa Major.

Delmarva Peninsula
1. The ___ comprises most of Delaware and parts of Maryland and Virginia.
2. Dover is the largest city of the ___ in terms of area; however, the commercial center of the ___ is Salisbury, Maryland.

Dover
1. ___ is the capital; it is the second largest city of Delaware in terms of population.
2. Although its population is less than that of Wilmington, ___ is the largest city in terms of area.

Du Pont
1. In the early 20th century the ___ family and their gunpowder company dominated Delaware's development.
2. Several members of the ___ family used their wealth to benefit the state. For example, Pierre S. ___ paid for the construction of new schools throughout the state.

Highest Point
1. Ebright Azimuth is the ___ in the state. It is located on Ebright Road, near the Pennsylvania state line.
2. The ___ in Delaware is only about 450 feet above sea level. It is in the Piedmont Region.

Executive Branch
1. The ___ includes the governor, lieutenant governor, attorney general, auditor of accounts, insurance commissioner, state treasurer, and various agencies.
2. The ___ enforces the laws and runs the day-to-day operations of the state.

Flag
1. The state ___ has a buff diamond on a field of colonial blue. Buff and colonial blue are the official state colors.
2. The state's coat of arms is in the center of the ___'s buff diamond.

Thomas Garrett
1. ___ is said to have helped more than 2,700 slaves escape to freedom in his 40 years as a "station master" on the Underground Railroad.
2. In 1848 ___ was tried and convicted for helping a slave family escape from Maryland.

Governor
1. The ___ is head of the executive branch of state government.
2. The present-day ___ is [fill in].

Greenwich Loam
1. ___ is the state soil.
2. This soil type is found in all counties of Delaware and is considered prime farmland.

Delaware Bingo

© Barbara M. Peller

Grey Fox 1. The ___ is the state wildlife animal. 2. This swift canine can run up to 28 miles per hours. It is the only canine able to climb trees.	**Holly** 1. The American ___ is the state tree. It has dark, thorny foliage and red berries. Its branches are often used as decorations during the Christmas and New Year holidays. 2. The American ___ is one of Delaware's most important forest trees.
Industry (-ies) 1. The manufacture of chemicals is the most important ___ in the state. 2. Food processing, agriculture and tourism are important ___.	**Judicial Branch** 1. The ___ interprets what our laws mean and makes decisions about the laws and those who break them. 2. It is made up of several courts, the highest of which is the Delaware Supreme Court.
Lady Bug(s) 1. The ___ is the state bug. ___ help gardeners and farmers by eating insect pests that damage plants. 2. The lady beetle, or ___ , is a beneficial insect because it eats so many aphids.	**Legislative Branch** 1. The General Assembly is the ___ of government; it comprises the Senate and the House of Representatives. 2. The ___ makes the laws.
Lewes 1. ___, Delaware, is located where the Delaware Bay and the Atlantic Ocean meet; the area is known as Cape Henlopen. 2. The Cape May-___ Ferry provides a 17-mile, 85-minute cruise between New Jersey and Delaware.	**Middle Atlantic** 1. Delaware is one of the ___ States. 2. Most sources include New Jersey, New York, Pennsylvania, Delaware and Maryland in this region.
Milk 1. Delaware is one of 20 states to select ___ as its state beverage. 2. ___ has been called a nearly perfect food; it is a source of protein, calcium, and other important nutrients.	**Motto** 1. "Liberty and Independence" is the state ___. 2. The state ___ appears on the state flag; it is on the ribbon at the base of the coat of arms.

Delaware Bingo

New Castle 1. On June 15, 1776, the Assembly of the Three Lower Counties met in the ___ Court House; New Castle, Kent, and Sussex counties declared their independence from Pennsylvania and England. 2. ___ was Delaware's first capital.	**Nickname** 1. The official ___ is The First State. 2. An old ___ was The Diamond State. It originated with Thomas Jefferson, who compared Delaware to a diamond—small but very valuable.
Caesar Rodney 1. This Patriot is depicted on horseback on the Delaware state quarter. 2. This Patriot rode through thunderstorms and severe heat on his way to Philadelphia to cast the deciding vote for independence.	**Peach** 1. This fruit was introduced to Delaware during colonial times. ___ farming is an important part of Delaware's agricultural heritage. 2. ___ pie is the official state dessert.
Peach Blossom 1. The ___ is the official state flower. 2. The ___ is the official state floral emblem.	**Piedmont** 1. A very small area of the northern part of the state lies in this geographic area. 2. The ___ is only about 10 miles wide at its widest point within the state. This region is marked by rolling hills.
River(s) 1. The Delaware ___ was named by the English after Sir Thomas West, 3rd Baron De La Warr. The Delaware Indians and the state were both named after the ___. 2. Delaware, Mispillion, and Nanticoke are ___ in Delaware.	**Seal** 1. A farmer and a militiaman are on the Great ___ of Delaware. 2. A sheaf of wheat, an ear of corn, an ox, and a sailing ship are all depicted on the Great ___.
Sillimanite 1. ___ is the state mineral. 2. This mineral is abundant in the metamorphic rocks of the Delaware Piedmont.	**Song** 1. "Our Delaware" is the state ___. It contains three verses, each in honor of a different county. 2. The first line of the state ___ is "Oh the hills of dear New Castle."

Delaware Bingo

Stonefly
1. The ___ is the state macroinvertebrate. It is one of 3 insects adopted as official symbols. The other two are the tiger swallowtail butterfly and the lady bug.
2. This insect was chosen as the official state macroinvertebrate because it is an indicator of the excellent water quality in the state.

Strawberry (-ies)
1. The ___ is the state fruit.
2. Delaware ___ are bred for taste rather than size. The ___ is an important agricultural product.

Sweet Goldenrod
1. ___ is the state herb.
2. Tea made from ___ has medicinal properties. It is useful in the treatment of coughs and colds, among other ailments.

Three Lower Counties
1. Documents from the early Revolutionary period referred to the area of Pennsylvania that is now Delaware as the ___ on the Delaware River.
2. On June 15, 1776, the Assembly of the ___ met in the New Castle Court House and declared their independence from Pennsylvania and England.

Tiger Swallowtail
1. The ___ is the state butterfly.
2. The male ___ has yellow and black striped markings on its wings and body. Some females are brown or black.

Underground Railroad
1. The ___ was a series of safe houses; "conductors" helped slaves escape from slavery to the North or to abolitionists in the South.
2. Delaware was a critical part of the journey to freedom via the ___. More than 3,000 slaves escaped through Delaware.

University of Delaware
1. The main campus of the ___ is located in Newark. It was founded in 1743.
2. The ___'s athletic teams are called the Fightin' Blue Hens.

Weakfish
1. The ___ was chosen as the state fish because of its value as a game and food fish.
2. The ___ is known by several different names. It got this name because its weak mouth muscles can cause a hook to tear free, allowing it to escape.

Wilmington
1. ___ is the largest city in Delaware.
2. Along with Philadelphia, Pennsylvania, and Camden, New Jersey, ___ is a major city in the Delaware Valley Metropolitan Area.

Winterthur
1. Founded by Henry Francis du Pont, ___ is a museum of American decorative arts.
2. ___ was once the 175-room childhood home of Henry Francis du Pont. It is situated on almost 1,000 acres, including 60 acres of naturalistic gardens.

Delaware Bingo

Delaware Bingo

Seal	Atlantic Coastal Plain	Belemnite(s)	Governor	Border (-ed)
Flag	Battle of Cooch's Bridge	Weakfish	Motto	Stonefly
University of Delaware	Milk		Peach Blossom	Wilmington
Underground Railroad	Song	Tiger Swallowtail	Middle Atlantic	Nickname
Peach	Holly	Du Pont	Sweet Goldenrod	Lady Bug(s)

Delaware Bingo: Card No. 1

Delaware Bingo

Underground Railroad	University of Delaware	Judicial Branch	Sillimanite	Lewes
Nickname	Highest Point	Constitution	Song	Caesar Rodney
Crab(s)	Holly		Industry (-ies)	Tiger Swallowtail
Piedmont	River(s)	Milk	Winterthur	Border (-ed)
Stonefly	Weakfish	Du Pont	Flag	Sweet Goldenrod

Delaware Bingo: Card No. 2

Delaware Bingo

Holly	Tiger Swallowtail	Highest Point	Middle Atlantic	University of Delaware
Nickname	Battle of Cooch's Bridge	Counties	Atlantic Coastal Plain	Grey Fox
Song	Weakfish		Caesar Rodney	Blue Hen(s)
Milk	Crab(s)	Peach	Piedmont	Judicial Branch
Sweet Goldenrod	Delaware Diamond	Du Pont	Winterthur	Lewes

Delaware Bingo

Milk	Caesar Rodney	Belemnite(s)	Delaware Diamond	Lewes
New Castle	Climate	Atlantic Coastal Plain	Sillimanite	University of Delaware
Peach Blossom	Piedmont		Lady Bug(s)	Governor
Tiger Swallowtail	Battle of Cooch's Bridge	Weakfish	Du Pont	Constitution
Delmarva Peninsula	Stonefly	Civil War	Sweet Goldenrod	Wilmington

Delaware Bingo: Card No. 4

Delaware Bingo

Stonefly	Border (-ed)	Song	Constitution	Delaware Diamond
New Castle	Tiger Swallowtail	Counties	Industry (-ies)	Battle of Cooch's Bridge
Belemnite(s)	Wilmington		Motto	Greenwich Loam
Lady Bug(s)	Lewes	Seal	Winterthur	Dover
Highest Point	Du Pont	University of Delaware	Milk	Peach Blossom

Delaware Bingo

Blue Hen(s)	Caesar Rodney	Judicial Branch	Lewes	Wilmington
Middle Atlantic	Song	Dover	Atlantic Coastal Plain	University of Delaware
Sillimanite	Delmarva Peninsula		Climate	Industry (-ies)
Du Pont	Peach	Winterthur	Civil War	Belemnite(s)
Nickname	Constitution	Seal	Peach Blossom	Executive Branch

Delaware Bingo: Card No. 6

Delaware Bingo

Seal	Caesar Rodney	Greenwich Loam	Tiger Swallowtail	Highest Point
Nickname	Lewes	Holly	Battle of Cooch's Bridge	New Castle
Wilmington	Governor		Industry (-ies)	Climate
Milk	Piedmont	Counties	Underground Railroad	Crab(s)
Du Pont	Delaware Diamond	Winterthur	Civil War	Blue Hen(s)

Delaware Bingo

Peach Blossom	Caesar Rodney	Thomas Garrett	Middle Atlantic	Climate
New Castle	Belemnite(s)	Sillimanite	Wilmington	Constitution
Executive Branch	Delaware Diamond		Lewes	Border (-ed)
Sweet Goldenrod	Milk	Underground Railroad	Delmarva Peninsula	Piedmont
Weakfish	Du Pont	Civil War	Song	Nickname

Delaware Bingo

Industry (-ies)	Highest Point	Holly	Executive Branch	Delaware Diamond
Delmarva Peninsula	Lewes	Peach Blossom	Song	Caesar Rodney
Grey Fox	Seal		Battle of Cooch's Bridge	Thomas Garrett
Dover	Border (-ed)	Peach	Motto	Greenwich Loam
Piedmont	Winterthur	Counties	Underground Railroad	Lady Bug(s)

Delaware Bingo

Underground Railroad	Middle Atlantic	Climate	Sillimanite	Executive Branch
Wilmington	Constitution	Atlantic Coastal Plain	Battle of Cooch's Bridge	Lewes
Delaware Diamond	Caesar Rodney		Governor	Crab(s)
Peach	Lady Bug(s)	Dover	Winterthur	Grey Fox
Counties	Nickname	Judicial Branch	Stonefly	Peach Blossom

Delaware Bingo

Blue Hen(s)	Caesar Rodney	Song	Dover	Nickname
Thomas Garrett	Grey Fox	Motto	Industry (-ies)	Atlantic Coastal Plain
New Castle	Lewes		Judicial Branch	Holly
Counties	University of Delaware	Winterthur	Delaware Diamond	Underground Railroad
Delmarva Peninsula	Du Pont	Seal	Civil War	Highest Point

Delaware Bingo

Highest Point	Border (-ed)	Grey Fox	Middle Atlantic	Industry (-ies)
Holly	Nickname	Belemnite(s)	Civil War	Battle of Cooch's Bridge
Seal	Greenwich Loam		Wilmington	Sillimanite
Du Pont	Piedmont	Lewes	Underground Railroad	New Castle
Caesar Rodney	Thomas Garrett	Delaware Diamond	Delmarva Peninsula	Constitution

Delaware Bingo

Dover	Border (-ed)	Blue Hen(s)	Grey Fox	Wilmington
Belemnite(s)	Thomas Garrett	Lewes	Industry (-ies)	Crab(s)
Middle Atlantic	Constitution		Holly	Greenwich Loam
Peach Blossom	Winterthur	Climate	Delaware Diamond	Underground Railroad
Du Pont	Lady Bug(s)	Civil War	Seal	Motto

Delaware Bingo

Flag	Lewes	Song	Industry (-ies)	Delmarva Peninsula
Constitution	Seal	Grey Fox	Battle of Cooch's Bridge	Caesar Rodney
Dover	Governor		Judicial Branch	Counties
Lady Bug(s)	Winterthur	Delaware Diamond	Climate	Blue Hen(s)
Du Pont	Sillimanite	Crab(s)	Nickname	Peach Blossom

Delaware Bingo

Motto	Industry (-ies)	Song	Highest Point	Middle Atlantic
Blue Hen(s)	Judicial Branch	Atlantic Coastal Plain	Belemnite(s)	Delmarva Peninsula
Wilmington	Seal		University of Delaware	Caesar Rodney
Du Pont	Grey Fox	Thomas Garrett	Winterthur	Dover
Nickname	Piedmont	Civil War	Executive Branch	Holly

Delaware Bingo

Climate	Grey Fox	Thomas Garrett	Executive Branch	River(s)
Sillimanite	Crab(s)	Greenwich Loam	New Castle	Governor
Dover	Border (-ed)		Wilmington	Holly
Milk	Constitution	Du Pont	Motto	Underground Railroad
Delmarva Peninsula	Three Lower Counties	Civil War	Piedmont	Caesar Rodney

Delaware Bingo: Card No. 16

Delaware Bingo

Counties	Strawberry (-ies)	Legislative Branch	Grey Fox	Flag
Motto	Delmarva Peninsula	Winterthur	Governor	Greenwich Loam
Industry (-ies)	Peach Blossom		Three Lower Counties	Thomas Garrett
Lady Bug(s)	Nickname	Underground Railroad	Song	Crab(s)
Peach	Dover	Highest Point	Middle Atlantic	Border (-ed)

Delaware Bingo

Executive Branch	Delaware Diamond	Constitution	Dover	Sillimanite
Caesar Rodney	Counties	Peach	Wilmington	Delmarva Peninsula
Industry (-ies)	Crab(s)		Legislative Branch	Belemnite(s)
Border (-ed)	Atlantic Coastal Plain	Winterthur	Underground Railroad	Judicial Branch
Three Lower Counties	Grey Fox	Song	Strawberry (-ies)	Blue Hen(s)

Delaware Bingo: Card No. 18

Delaware Bingo

Wilmington	Blue Hen(s)	Grey Fox	Thomas Garrett	Underground Railroad
Motto	Middle Atlantic	Caesar Rodney	Highest Point	Governor
Strawberry (-ies)	Delaware Diamond		Battle of Cooch's Bridge	University of Delaware
Judicial Branch	Three Lower Counties	Peach	Piedmont	Legislative Branch
Belemnite(s)	River(s)	Nickname	Peach Blossom	Civil War

Delaware Bingo

Flag	Strawberry (-ies)	Middle Atlantic	Grey Fox	Civil War
Constitution	Holly	New Castle	Peach	Sillimanite
Border (-ed)	Greenwich Loam		Milk	Atlantic Coastal Plain
Stonefly	Weakfish	Sweet Goldenrod	Piedmont	Three Lower Counties
Tiger Swallowtail	Peach Blossom	River(s)	Underground Railroad	Legislative Branch

Delaware Bingo: Card No. 20

Delaware Bingo

Motto	Blue Hen(s)	New Castle	Grey Fox	Stonefly
Border (-ed)	Legislative Branch	Climate	Thomas Garrett	Seal
Crab(s)	Nickname		Strawberry (-ies)	Song
Peach	Highest Point	Three Lower Counties	Lady Bug(s)	Peach Blossom
Milk	River(s)	Civil War	Counties	Piedmont

Delaware Bingo: Card No. 21

Delaware Bingo

Executive Branch	Judicial Branch	Legislative Branch	Belemnite(s)	Dover
Sillimanite	Middle Atlantic	University of Delaware	Thomas Garrett	Battle of Cooch's Bridge
Constitution	Governor		Seal	Greenwich Loam
Three Lower Counties	Lady Bug(s)	Piedmont	Atlantic Coastal Plain	New Castle
River(s)	Counties	Strawberry (-ies)	Crab(s)	Motto

Delaware Bingo

Climate	Strawberry (-ies)	Highest Point	Belemnite(s)	Civil War
Blue Hen(s)	Flag	Nickname	Motto	Atlantic Coastal Plain
Judicial Branch	Dover		Sweet Goldenrod	Seal
Crab(s)	River(s)	Three Lower Counties	Counties	Piedmont
Stonefly	Weakfish	Peach Blossom	Peach	Legislative Branch

Delaware Bingo

Climate	Peach Blossom	Flag	Strawberry (-ies)	Thomas Garrett
Legislative Branch	Civil War	New Castle	Sillimanite	Seal
Greenwich Loam	Executive Branch		Dover	Crab(s)
Stonefly	Sweet Goldenrod	Three Lower Counties	Counties	Border (-ed)
Tiger Swallowtail	Milk	River(s)	Middle Atlantic	Weakfish

Delaware Bingo

Milk	New Castle	Strawberry (-ies)	Song	Legislative Branch
Atlantic Coastal Plain	Border (-ed)	Motto	Climate	Battle of Cooch's Bridge
Lady Bug(s)	Thomas Garrett		Sweet Goldenrod	Three Lower Counties
University of Delaware	Stonefly	Weakfish	River(s)	Governor
Civil War	Flag	Constitution	Delmarva Peninsula	Tiger Swallowtail

Delaware Bingo: Card No. 25

Delaware Bingo

Legislative Branch	Strawberry (-ies)	Judicial Branch	Sillimanite	Executive Branch
Peach	Middle Atlantic	Thomas Garrett	Flag	Climate
Lady Bug(s)	Sweet Goldenrod		Governor	Milk
Counties	Belemnite(s)	Stonefly	River(s)	Three Lower Counties
Greenwich Loam	Delmarva Peninsula	Song	Weakfish	Tiger Swallowtail

Delaware Bingo

Judicial Branch	Constitution	Strawberry (-ies)	Flag	Holly
Stonefly	Sweet Goldenrod	Motto	Three Lower Counties	Battle of Cooch's Bridge
Winterthur	Weakfish		River(s)	Milk
Executive Branch	Blue Hen(s)	New Castle	Tiger Swallowtail	Atlantic Coastal Plain
Delmarva Peninsula	Governor	Legislative Branch	University of Delaware	Greenwich Loam

Delaware Bingo

Judicial Branch	Flag	University of Delaware	Strawberry (-ies)	Climate
Holly	Legislative Branch	Sweet Goldenrod	Sillimanite	Governor
Weakfish	Crab(s)		Greenwich Loam	Peach
Underground Railroad	Executive Branch	Nickname	River(s)	Three Lower Counties
Belemnite(s)	Industry (-ies)	Delmarva Peninsula	Tiger Swallowtail	Stonefly

Delaware Bingo

Legislative Branch	Flag	Executive Branch	Motto	Industry (-ies)
Piedmont	Peach	New Castle	Greenwich Loam	University of Delaware
Lady Bug(s)	Sweet Goldenrod		Battle of Cooch's Bridge	Strawberry (-ies)
Holly	Stonefly	Lewes	River(s)	Three Lower Counties
Climate	Thomas Garrett	Tiger Swallowtail	Blue Hen(s)	Weakfish

Delaware Bingo

Delaware Diamond	Strawberry (-ies)	Sillimanite	Industry (-ies)	Three Lower Counties
Atlantic Coastal Plain	Flag	Judicial Branch	Governor	Battle of Cooch's Bridge
Lady Bug(s)	Dover		Greenwich Loam	New Castle
Tiger Swallowtail	Blue Hen(s)	Belemnite(s)	River(s)	Sweet Goldenrod
Stonefly	Wilmington	Weakfish	Legislative Branch	University of Delaware

Delaware Bingo: Card No. 30